ALSO BY FLANNERY O'CONNOR

NOVELS
Wise Blood
The Violent Bear It Away

STORIES
A Good Man Is Hard to Find
Everything That Rises Must Converge
The Complete Stories

NONFICTION
Mystery and Manners
The Habit of Being

A PRAYER
JOURNAL

A PRAYER
JOURNAL

✠

FLANNERY
O'CONNOR

FARRAR, STRAUS AND GIROUX

NEW YORK

Farrar, Straus and Giroux
18 West 18th Street, New York 10011

An excerpt from *A Prayer Journal* originally appeared in *The New Yorker.*

Library of Congress Cataloging-in-Publication Data
O'Connor, Flannery.
    A prayer journal / Flannery O'Connor ; edited and with an introduction
by W. A. Sessions. — 1st [edition].
        pages   cm
    ISBN 978-0-374-23691-5
    1. Catholic Church—Prayers and devotions.   2. Spiritual journals.
3. O'Connor, Flannery—Religion.   I. Sessions, William A., editor of
compilation.   II. Title.

BX2182.3 .O35 2013
282.092—dc23

                                                                    2013021681

Designed by Jonathan D. Lippincott

www.fsgbooks.com
www.twitter.com/fsgbooks • www.facebook.com/fsgbooks

5   7   9   10   8   6   4

CONTENTS

INTRODUCTION

BY W. A. SESSIONS

From January 1946 to September 1947, Flannery O'Connor kept a journal that was, in essence, a series of prayers. She was not twenty-one years of age when she began this journal, and at twenty-two, when she wrote the last entry, it was clear that her prayer journal had already made a difference in her life.

In this journal, written in Iowa City, where she had initially gone to study journalism but ended up in writing workshops, O'Connor reckoned with her new life. Here, she consecrated herself to a force that had surrounded her, so she believed, since her birth, in Savannah, Georgia, on March 25, 1925. Iowa City, in the American heartland, seemed the polar opposite of the racially mixed but segregated port city, which in her time was exotic (the last great port southward, before Cuba and the Caribbean). For her, Savannah had opened up more than the diversity of human existence. There a series of Catholic rituals and teachings had offered her young life a coherent universe. By 1946, Savannah had for O'Connor ceded to the university world of Iowa, where new influences, including intellectual joys, brought with them questions and skepticism.

In that freedom, O'Connor began her journal and initiated a rare colloquy. She began to compose entries that soon transcended simple meditations on the perplexities of life. From the start (we do not have the first pages) the journal contained lyric outcries that became a singular dialogue. In fact, she seemed to be inventing her own prayer form. Abrupt, truncated, and serial, the individual entries convey great intensity: "Oh Lord," she cries out toward the end of the journal, "make me a mystic, immediately." This urgency was present even in her final cry of disappointment. By then she knew that she would not have an immediate answer from the object of her love—at least not on her own terms. She would have to wait patiently in a world of triviality, and even of the "erotic," until "the Lord's" responses came.

Such journal entries were not as spontaneous as they might seem. Even at twenty-one, O'Connor was a craftswoman of the first order, and the facsimile that appears in this volume reveals her careful emendations. To dramatize her desire—and she was foremost a dramatic writer—she recognized that she must not report, but "render," in the Jamesian manner she was learning at Iowa. Her letters of action, written in search of her lover, became entries in a journal. The entries themselves could be simple, intimate, at moments childlike. At the same time, they could dramatize desires that were Olympian, astonishing for their range and depth of observation about human life and destiny—and perhaps too astonishing for earlier readers and guardians of the sheaf of handwritten pages buried for more than half a century.

But to whom did she write these letters, these entries? Who was this lover she identified as such? In the journal, she generally named this presence God. She called him "Father" only in connection with a Gospel quotation, and she made only a few direct references in the whole journal to "Christ"—the most direct an impassioned petition: "I don't want to be doomed to mediocrity in my feeling for Christ. I want to feel. I want to love. Take me, dear Lord, and set me in the direction I am to go." Her love was universal and, like Moses's burning bush, alive and on fire.

In fact, if her love represented an absolute, the writer herself existed, as O'Connor's allusions in her journal emphasize, in a real, deeply human world. God and humanity were not mutually exclusive terms, of course, and the young writer understood her daily world as a particular moment in history, its center always in that lover she felt seeking her as she sought him in the midst of a bustling Iowa City in the latter part of the 1940s. GIs were returning from war for their free education, and the streets were packed with students. Remarkably, for O'Connor, even African Americans were there without apparent social restrictions. One of her closer creative-writing friends, a young woman, Gloria Bremerwell, with whom she had dinner many times, was African American. O'Connor may not have known that there were no barbershops in Iowa City where black males could get their hair cut at the time.

The prayers in her journal naturally emerged out of the busy classrooms, libraries, and streets of Iowa City. Her dorm room, which opened onto the only bathroom on the floor, was far from private. In that awkward room the young writer began her journal as she sat at a desk with her pens, pencils, and typewriter beside her hot plate (all the refrigerated items stood outside the window). Thus her world was far from cloistered. Yet in her years at Iowa she was increasingly seeing openings both out of and into her life—and her desire to write fiction carried the greatest meaning for her in such a setting, where so many influences converged.

In fact, in the midst of writing these prayers, she began her first novel, eventually titled *Wise Blood*. That was during the Thanksgiving break of 1946, and whatever else the outreach of prayer had done, in initiating this truly original work of American fiction, O'Connor had extended the reach of her journal. Her prayer to be a good writer—reiterated often in the journal—had already been answered. She had discovered within herself a deeper source for acts of her imagination. Indeed, she had learned there in Iowa how Coleridge's act of imagination as the "willing suspension of disbelief" could become for her the freedom of creating fiction in that suspension.

By the time O'Connor wrote her final journal entry, she had offered herself directly to God. In her entries she sought to consecrate herself so that she might love the absolute more, sacrifice more. But on September 26, 1947, three years before the sudden arrival of lupus, the disease that had killed her father and would kill her, the young O'Connor wrote her last entry. Nothing appeared to have happened. On that day her "thoughts are so far away from God," and she wondered in a discordant image if the "feeling I egg up writing here" was little more than "a sham." That very day, in fact, she had proved herself "a glutton—for Scotch oatmeal cookies and erotic thought." She closed the journal matter-of-factly: "There is nothing left to say of me."

Actually there was a great deal left. The journal itself was finished, and it accurately reflected O'Connor's literary achievements thus far and even foretold her suffering and death. Not least were the results of her outlandish hope, at least in the twentieth century, for total commitment to God. In that hope she had created characters who knew (negatively, like the Misfit of "A Good Man Is Hard to Find," or positively, like the tattooed man of "Parker's Back" or Ruby Turpin of "Revelation") the cost of having a destiny painful to wait out but, in her fiction, alive only through their waiting.

Before Christmas of 1950, O'Connor traveled alone

by train from Connecticut to Georgia. Her friend Sally Fitzgerald saw the "active young woman with a bright beret" off at the station. But by the time O'Connor arrived in Atlanta, she looked drawn and bent, "like an old man," according to her waiting uncle. In the course of her journey from North to South, O'Connor had had her first attack of lupus, the disease that afflicted her until her death in 1964, at age thirty-nine. Paradoxically, those years of suffering became the most fertile for her writing, and she produced some of the greatest fiction in American literature. Ironically, the prayers of her journal had been answered.

EDITOR'S NOTE

Flannery O'Connor considered herself "a very innocent speller." Spelling has therefore been corrected in this transcription of *A Prayer Journal*, so that the reader is not distracted. O'Connor's punctuation is followed as faithfully as legibility would allow, with certain bracketed exceptions. Those interested in examining the original text may find it at the back of this volume, in O'Connor's own hand.

A PRAYER
JOURNAL

[UNDATED ENTRIES]

[. . .]* effort at artistry in this rather than thinking of You and feeling inspired with the love I wish I had.

Dear God, I cannot love Thee the way I want to. You are the slim crescent of a moon that I see and my self is the earth's shadow that keeps me from seeing all the moon. The crescent is very beautiful and perhaps that is all one like I am should or could see; but what I am afraid of, dear God, is that my self shadow will grow so large that it blocks the whole moon, and that I will judge myself by the shadow that is nothing.

I do not know You God because I am in the way. Please help me to push myself aside.

I want very much to succeed in the world with what I want to do. I have prayed to You about this with my mind and my nerves on it and strung my nerves into a tension over it and said, "oh God please," and "I must," and "please, please." I have not asked You, I feel, in the

*The opening pages of the journal appear to have been lost.

right way. Let me henceforth ask you with resignation—that not being or meant to be a slacking up in prayer but a less frenzied kind—realizing that the frenzy is caused by an eagerness for what I want and not a spiritual trust. I do not wish to presume. I want to love.

Oh God please make my mind clear.

Please make it clean.

I ask You for a greater love for my holy Mother and I ask her for a greater love for You.

Please help me to get down under things and find where You are.

I do not mean to deny the traditional prayers I have said all my life; but I have been saying them and not feeling them. My attention is always very fugitive. This way I have it every instant. I can feel a warmth of love heating me when I think & write this to You. Please do not let the explanations of the psychologists about this make it turn suddenly cold. My intellect is so limited, Lord, that I can only trust in You to preserve me as I should be.

Please help all the ones I love to be free from their suffering. Please forgive me.

My dear God, I am impressed with how much I have to be thankful for in a material sense; and in a spiritual sense I have the opportunity of being even more fortunate. But it seems apparent to me that I am not translating this opportunity into fact. You say, dear God, to ask for grace and it will be given. I ask for it. I realize that there is more to it than that—that I have to behave like I want it. "Not those who say, Lord, Lord, but those who do the Will of My Father." Please help me to know the will of my Father—not a scrupulous nervousness nor yet a lax presumption but a clear, reasonable knowledge; and after this give me a strong Will to be able to bend it to the Will of the Father.

Please let Christian principles permeate my writing and please let there be enough of my writing (published) for Christian principles to permeate. I dread, Oh Lord, losing my faith. My mind is not strong. It is a prey to all sorts of intellectual quackery. I do not want it to be fear which keeps me in the church. I don't want to be a coward, staying with You because I fear hell. I should reason that if I fear hell, I can be assured of the author of it. But learned people can analyze for me why I fear hell and their implication is that there is no hell. But I believe in hell. Hell seems a great deal more feasible to my weak mind than heaven. No doubt because hell is a more earthly-seeming thing. I can fancy the tortures of the damned but I cannot imagine the disembodied souls hanging in a crystal for all eternity praising God. It is natural that I should not imagine this. If we could accurately map heaven some of our up-&-coming scientists would begin drawing blueprints for its improvement, and the bourgeois would sell guides 10¢ the copy to all over 65. But I do not mean to be clever although I do mean to be clever on 2nd thought and like to be clever & want to be considered so. But the point more specifically here is, I don't want to fear to be out, I want to love to be in; I don't want to believe in hell but in heaven. Stating this does me no good. It is a matter of the gift of grace. Help me to feel that I will give up every earthly thing for this. I do not mean becoming a nun.

My dear God, how stupid we people are until You give us something. Even in praying it is You who have to pray in us. I would like to write a beautiful prayer but I have nothing to do it from. There is a whole sensible world around me that I should be able to turn to Your praise; but I cannot do it. Yet at some insipid moment when I may possibly be thinking of floor wax or pigeon eggs, the opening of a beautiful prayer may come up from my subconscious and lead me to write something exalted. I am not a philosopher or I could understand these things.

If I knew all of myself dear God, if I could discover everything in me pedantic egocentric, in any way insincere, what would I be then? But what would I do about those feelings that are now fear, now joy, that lie too deep to be touched by my understanding. I am afraid of insidious hands Oh Lord which grope into the darkness of my soul. Please be my guard against them. Please be the Cover at the top of the passage. Am I keeping my faith by laziness, dear God? But that is an idea that would appeal to someone who could only think.

My dear God, I do not want this to be a metaphysical exercise but something in praise of God. It is probably more liable to being therapeutical than metaphysical, with the element of self underlying its thoughts. Prayers should be composed I understand of adoration, contrition, thanksgiving, and supplication and I would like to see what I can do with each without writing an exegesis. It is the adoration of You, dear God, that most dismays me. I cannot comprehend the exaltation that must be due You. Intellectually, I assent: let us adore God. But can we do that without feeling? To feel, we must know. And for this, when it is practically impossible for us to get it ourselves, not completely, of course, but what we can, we are dependent on God. We are dependent on God for our adoration of Him, adoration, that is, in the fullest sense of the term. Give me the grace, dear God, to adore You for even this I cannot do for myself. Give me the grace to adore You with the excitement of the old priests when they sacrificed a lamb to You. Give me the grace to adore

You with the awe that fills Your priests when they sacrifice the Lamb on our altars. Give me the grace to be
impatient for the time when I shall see You face to face
and need no stimulus than that to adore You. Give me
the grace, dear God, to see the bareness and the misery
of the places where You are not adored but desecrated.

Dear God, I am so discouraged about my work. I have the feeling of discouragement that is. I realize I don't know what I realize. Please help me dear God to be a good writer and to get something else accepted. That is so far from what I deserve, of course, that I am naturally struck with the nerve of it. Contrition in me is largely imperfect. I don't know if I've ever been sorry for a sin because it hurt You. That kind of contrition is better than none but it is selfish. To have the other kind, it is necessary to have knowledge, faith extraordinary. All boils down to grace, I suppose. Again asking God to help us be sorry for having hurt Him. I am afraid of pain and I suppose that is what we have to have to get grace. Give me the courage to stand the pain to get the grace, Oh Lord. Help me with this life that seems so treacherous, so disappointing.

Dear God, tonight it is not disappointing because you have given me a story. Don't let me ever think, dear God, that I was anything but the instrument for Your story— just like the typewriter was mine. Please let the story, dear God, in its revisions, be made too clear for any false & low interpretation because in it, I am not trying to disparage anybody's religion although when it was coming out, I didn't know exactly what I was trying to do or what it was going to mean. I don't know now if it is consistent. Please don't let me have to scrap the story because it turns out to mean more wrong than right—or any wrong. I want it to mean that the good in man sometimes shows through his commercialism but that it is not the fault of the commercialism that it does.

Perhaps the idea would be that good can show through even something that is cheap. I don't know, but dear God, I wish you would take care of making it a sound story because I don't know how, just like I didn't know how to write it but it came. Anyway it all brings me to thanksgiving, the third thing to include in prayer. When I think of all I have to be thankful for I wonder that You don't just kill me now because You've done so much for me already & I haven't been particularly grateful. My thanksgiving is never in the form of self sacrifice—a few memorized prayers babbled once over lightly. All this disgusts me in myself but does not fill me with the poignant feeling I should have to adore You with, to be sorry with, or to thank You with. Perhaps the feeling I keep asking for, is something again selfish—something to help me to feel that everything with <u>me</u> is all right. And yet it seems only natural but maybe being thus natural is being thus selfish. My mind is a most insecure thing, not to be depended on. It gives me scruples at one minute & leaves me lax the next. If I must know all these things thru the mind, dear Lord, please strengthen mine. Thank you, dear God, I believe I do feel thankful for all You've done for me. I want to. I do. And thank my dear Mother whom I do love, Our Lady of Perpetual Help.

My dear God, Supplication. This is the only one of the four I am competent in. It takes no supernatural grace to ask for what one wants and I have asked You bountifully, oh Lord. I believe it is right to ask You too and to ask our Mother to ask You, but I don't want to overemphasize this angle of my prayers. Help me to ask You, oh Lord, for what is good for me to have, for what I can have and do Your service by having.

I have been reading Mr. Kafka and I feel his problem of getting grace. But I see it doesn't have to be that way for the Catholic who can go to Communion every day. The Msgr. today said it was the business of reason, not emotion—the love of God. The emotion would be a help. I realized last time that it would be a selfish one. Oh dear God, the reason is very empty. I suppose mine is also lazy. But I want to get near You. Yet it seems almost a sin to suggest such a thing even. Perhaps Communion doesn't give the nearness I mean. The nearness I mean comes after death perhaps. It is what we are struggling for and if I found it either I would be dead or I would have seen it for a second and life would be intolerable. I don't know about this or anything. It sounds puerile my saying anything so obvious.

My dear God, to keep myself on a course, I am going to consider Faith, Hope, and Charity. Now Faith. Of the three, this gives me the most mental pain. At every point in this educational process, we are told that it is ridiculous and their arguments sound so good it is hard not to fall into them. The arguments might not sound so good to someone with a better mind; but my mental trappings are as they are, and I am always on the brink of assenting—it is almost a subconscious assent. Now how am I to remain faithful without cowardice when these conditions influence me like they do. I can't read the particular depths of myself that say something about this. There is something down there that is feeling—it is under the subconscious assent—in a certain way about this. It may be that which is holding me in. Dear God, please let it be that instead of that cowardice the psychologists would gloat so over & explain so glibly. And please don't let it be what they so jubilantly call water-tight-compartments. Dear Lord please give the people like me who don't have the brains to cope with that, please give us some kind of weapon, not to defend us from them but to defend us from ourselves after they have got through with us. Dear God, I don't want to have invented my faith to satisfy my weakness. I don't want to have created God to my own image as they're so fond of saying. Please give me the necessary grace, oh Lord, and please don't let it be as hard to get as Kafka made it.

Dear God, About hope, I am somewhat at a loss. It is so easy to say I hope to—the tongue slides over it. I think perhaps hope can only be realized by contrasting it with despair. And I am too lazy to despair. Please don't visit me with it, dear Lord, I would be so miserable. Hope, however, must be something distinct from faith. I unconsciously put it in the faith department. It must be something positive that I have never felt. It must be a positive force, else why the distinction between it and faith? I would like to order things so that I can feel all of a piece spiritually. I don't suppose I order things. But all my requests seem to melt down to one for grace—that supernatural grace that does whatever it does. My mind is in a little box, dear God, down inside other boxes inside other boxes and on and on. There is very little air in my box. Dear God, please give me as much air as it is not presumptuous to ask for. Please let some light shine out of all the things around me so that I can what it amounts to I suppose is be selfish. Is there no getting around that dear God? No escape from ourselves? Into something bigger? Oh dear God I want to write a novel, a good novel. I want to do this for a good feeling & for a bad one. The bad one is uppermost. The psychologists say it is the natural one. Let me get away dear God from all things thus "natural." Help me to get what is more than natural into my work—help me to love & bear with my work on that account. If I have to sweat for it, dear God, let it be as in Your service. I would like to be intelligently holy. I am a presumptuous fool, but maybe the vague thing in me that keeps me in is hope.

Dear God, In a way I got a good punishment for my lack of charity to Mr. Rothburg* last year. He came back at me today like a tornado which while it didn't hurt me too much yet ruined my show. All this is about charity. Dear Lord please make my mind vigilant about that. I say many many too many uncharitable things about people everyday. I say them because they make me look clever. Please help me to realize <u>practically</u> how cheap this is. I have nothing to be proud of yet myself. I am stupid, quite as stupid as the people I ridicule. Please help me to stop this selfishness because I love you, dear God. I don't want to be all excuses though. I am not much. Please help me to do Your Word oh Lord.

*A fellow workshop student.

11/4 [1946]

I have decided this is not much as a direct medium of prayer. Prayer is not even as premeditated as this—it is of the moment & this is too slow for the moment. I have started on a new phase of my spiritual life—I trust. Tied up with it, is the throwing off of certain adolescent habits & habits of mind. It does not take much to make us realize what fools we are, but the little it takes is long in coming. I see my ridiculous self by degrees. One thing I have seen this week—it has been a peculiar week—is my constant seeing of myself as what I want to be. Not the fulfillment of what I want to be, but the right genre, the correct embryo in the correct beast. The consequence of such a delightful state of coma will naturally be the eternal embryo—and eternal in no false sense. I must grow. I have a right I believe to show such interest in myself as long as my interest is in my immortal soul and what keeps it pure. "Save to the pure & in their purest hour," Coleridge wrote—the gift of imagination functioned only then, only for those. Start with the soul and

perhaps the temporal gifts I want to exercise will have
their chance; and if they do not, I have the best in my
hands already, the only thing really needed. God must
be in all my work. I have been reading Bernanos. It is so
very wonderful. Will I ever know anything?

11/6/

Mediocrity is a hard word to apply to oneself; yet I see myself so equal with it that it is impossible not to throw it at myself—realizing even as I do that I will be old & beaten before I accept it. I think to accept it would be to accept Despair. There must be some way for the naturally mediocre to escape it[.] The way must be Grace. There must be a way to escape it even when you know you are even below it. Perhaps knowing you are below it is a way to begin. I say I am equal with it; but I am below it. I will always be staggering between Despair & Presumption, facing first one & then the other, deciding which makes me look the best, which fits most comfortably, most conveniently. I'll never take a large chunk of anything. I'll nibble nervously here & there. Fear of God is right; but, God, it is not this nervousness[.] It is something huge, great, magnanimous. It must be a joy. Every virtue must be vigorous. Virtue must be the only vigorous thing in our lives. Sin is large & stale. You can never finish eating it nor ever digest it. It has to be vomited.

But perhaps that is too literary a statement—this mustn't get insincere.

How can I live—how shall I live. Obviously the only way to live right is to give up everything. But I have no vocation & maybe that is wrong anyway. But how [to] eliminate this picky fish bone kind of way I do things—I want so to love God all the way. At the same time I want all the things that seem opposed to it—I want to be a <u>fine</u> writer. Any success will tend to swell my head— unconsciously even. If I ever do get to be a fine writer, it will not be because I am a fine writer but because God has given me credit for a few of the things He kindly wrote for me. Right at present this does not seem to be His policy. I can't write a thing. But I'll continue to try— that is the point. And at every dry point, I will be reminded Who is doing the work when it is done & Who is not doing it at that moment. Right now I wonder if God will ever do any more writing for me. He has promised His grace; I am not so sure about the other. Perhaps I have not been thankful enough for what has gone before.

The desires of the flesh—excluding the stomach— have been taken away from me. For how long I don't know but I hope forever. It is a great peace to be rid of them.

Can't anyone teach me how to pray?

II/II

How hard it is to keep any one intention[,] any one attitude toward a piece of work[,] any one tone[,] any one anything. I find a certain peace in my soul these days that is very fine—lead us not into temptation. The story level, bah. Work, work, work. Dear God, let me work, keep me working, I want so to be able to work. If my sin is laziness I want to be able to conquer it.

I looked back over some of these entries.*

*The remaining text on this page of the journal appears to have been excised.

1/2/47

No one can be an atheist who does not know all things.
Only God is an atheist. The devil is the greatest believer
& he has his reasons.

I/II/47

Can we ever settle on calling ourselves mediocre—me on myself? If I am not this or that that someone else is, may I not be something else that I am that I cannot yet see fully or describe? I go back, and [. . .]

St. Thomas [. . .]*

Rousseau has it that the Protestant has to think; the Catholic to submit. It is presumed I suppose that ultimately the Protestant too has to submit; but the Catholic never to think, i.e., about the nature of man's relation to God. This is interesting. Catholicism being a guide book to the only means of communication is worth submitting to in the Catholic's view. And all these doctrines which deny submission deny God. Hell, a literal hell, is our only hope. Take it away & we will become wholly a wasteland not a half a one. Sin is a great thing as long as it's recognized. It leads a good many people to God who wouldn't get there otherwise. But cease to recognize it, or take it

*The remaining text on this page of the journal appears to have been excised.

away from devil as devil & give it to devil as psychologist, and you also take away God. If there is no sin in
this world there is no God in heaven. No heaven. There
are those who would have it that way. But even among
the literary now it is becoming popular to believe in
God. There is a certain shocking something about it. But
Catholics have to think certainly—as far as they are
able—or as far maybe as they want to only. Me. I have to
in an attempt to do this am I trying to shock with God?
Am I trying to push Him in there violently, feet foremost? Maybe that's all right. Maybe if I'm doing it it's all
right? Maybe I'm mediocre. I'd rather be less. I'd rather
be nothing. An imbecile. Yet this is wrong. Mediocrity, if
that is my scourge, is something I'll have to submit to.
If that is my scourge. If I ever find out will be time to
submit. I will have to have a good many opinions.

1/25/47

The majesty of my thoughts this evening! Do all these things read alike as they seem to? They all send a faint nausea thru me—albeit they were sincere at the time & I recant none of my articles of faith. This evening I picture theoretically myself at 70 saying it's done, it's finished, it's what it is, & being no nearer than I am. This moral turpitude at 70 won't be tolerable. I want a revolution now, a mild revolution, something that will put an even 20th cen. asceticism into me at least when I pass the grocery.

The intellectual & artistic delights God gives us are visions & like visions we pay for them; & the thirst for the vision doesn't necessarily carry with it a thirst for the attendant suffering. Looking back I have suffered, not my share, but enough to call it that but there's a terrific balance due. Dear God please send me Your Grace.

4/14/47

I must write down that I am to be an artist. Not in the sense of aesthetic frippery but in the sense of aesthetic craftsmanship; otherwise I will feel my loneliness continually—like this today. The word craftsmanship takes care of the work angle & the word aesthetic the truth angle. Angle. It will be a life struggle with no consummation. When something is finished, it cannot be possessed. Nothing can be possessed but the struggle. All our lives are consumed in possessing struggle but only when the struggle is cherished & directed to a final consummation outside of this life is it of any value. I want to be the best artist it is possible for me to be, under God.

I do not want to be lonely all my life but people only make us lonelier by reminding us of God. Dear God please help me to be an artist, please let it lead to You.

5/4

To maintain any thread in the novel there must be a view of the world behind it & the most important single item under this view of [the] world is conception of love— divine, natural, & perverted. It is probably possible to say that when a view of love is present—a broad enough view—no more need be added to make the worldview.

Freud, Proust, Lawrence have located love inside the human & there is no need to question their location; however, there is no need either to define love as they do—only as desire, since this precludes Divine Love, which, while it too may be desire, is a different kind of desire—Divine desire—and is outside of man and capable of lifting him up to itself. Man's desire for God is bedded in his unconscious & seeks to satisfy itself in physical possession of another human. This necessarily is a passing, fading attachment in its sensuous aspects since it is a poor substitute for what the unconscious is after. The more conscious the desire for God becomes the more successful union with another becomes because the intelligence realizes the relation in its relation to a greater desire & if this intelligence is in both parties the motive power in the desire for God becomes double & gains in becoming God-like. The modern man isolated from faith, from raising his desire for God into a conscious desire, is sunk into the position of seeing physical love as an end in itself. Thus his romanticizing it, wallowing in it, & then cynicizing it. Or in the case of the artist like Proust of his realizing that it is the only thing worth life but seeing it without purpose, accidental, and unsatisfying after desire has been fulfilled. Proust's conception of desire could only be that way since he makes it the highest point of existence—which it is—but with nothing supernatural to end in. It sinks lower & lower in the unconscious, to the very pit of it, which is Hell. Certainly hell is located in the unconscious even as the desire for God is. The desire for God may be in a super consciousness which is unconscious. Satan fell into his libido or his id whichever is the more complete Freudian term.

Perversion is the end result of denying or revolting against supernatural love, descending from the unconscious superconsciousness to the id. Where perversion is disease or result of disease, this does not apply since no free will operates. The Sex act is a religious act & when it occurs without God it is a mock act or at best an empty act. Proust is right that only a love which does not satisfy can continue. Two people can remain "in love"—a phrase made practically useless by stinking romanticism—only if their common desire for each other unites in a greater desire for God—i.e., they do not become satisfied but more desirous together of the supernatural love in union with God. My God, take these boils & blisters & warts of sick romanticism [. . .]*

*The following page of the journal has been excised.

5/30

Tore the last thing out. It was worthy of me all right; but not worthy of what I ought to be. Bloy has come my way. The awful thing is that we <u>can</u> go back to ourselves being ourselves after reading him. He is an iceberg hurled at me to break up my Titanic and I hope my Titanic will be smashed, but I am afraid it takes more than Bloy to destroy the age in us—the age is The Fall still I suppose and certainly Original Sin in us. Conquer it but can't throw it off, fight it and maim it but never kill it. It is hard to want to suffer; I presume Grace is necessary for the want. I am a mediocre of the spirit but there is hope. I am at least of the spirit and that means alive. What about these dead people I am living with? What about them? We who live will have to pay for their deaths. Being dead what can they do. It is for them, I presume, that the saints died. No, the saints died for God and God died for the dead. They didn't have to submit to God's indignity. No one can do again what Christ did. These modern "Christs" pictured on war posters & in poems—"every man is Jesus; every woman Mary"[—]would have made Bloy retch. The rest of us have lost our power to vomit.

9/22 and Bloy again. It should be a great instigator of humility in me that I am so lukewarm as to need Bloy always to send me into serious thought—and even then it is not sustained very long. The summer was very arid spiritually & up here getting to go to Mass again every day has left me unmoved—thoughts awful in their pettiness & selfishness come into my mind even with the Host on my tongue. Maybe the Lord had pity on me and sent me wandering down the stacks to pick up Pfleger on Bloy & Péguy and some others. It is terrible to think of my unconsciousness when I really know. Too weak to pray for suffering[,] too weak even to get out a prayer for anything much except trifles. I don't want to be doomed to mediocrity in my feeling for Christ. I want to feel. I want to love. Take me, dear Lord, and set me in the direction I am to go. My Lady of Perpetual Help, pray for me.

9/23

Dear Lord please make me want You. It would be the greatest bliss. Not just to want You when I think about You but to want You all the time, to think about You all the time, to have the want driving in me, to have it like a cancer in me. It would kill me like a cancer and that would be the Fulfillment. It is easy for this writing to show a want. There is a want but it is abstract and cold, a dead want that goes well into writing because writing is dead. Writing is dead. Art is dead, dead by nature, not killed by unkindness. I bring my dead want into the place[,] the dead place it shows up most easily, into writing. This has its purpose if by God's grace it will wake another soul; but it does me no good. The "life" it receives in writing is dead to me, the more so in that it looks alive—a horrible deception. But not to me who knows this. Oh Lord please make this dead desire living, living in life, living as it will probably have to live in suffering. I feel too mediocre now to suffer. If suffering came to me I would not even recognize it. Lord keep me. Mother help me.

9/24

Giving one Catholicity, God deprives one of the pleasure of looking for it but here again He has shown His mercy for such a one as myself—and for that matter for all contemporary Catholics—who, if it had not been given, would not have looked[.] It is certainly His provision for all mediocre souls—a tool for us; for Bloy's statue it is—how to call it? God on earth? God as nearly as we can get to Him on earth. I wish only that I were one of the strong. If I were that less would have been given me and I would have <u>felt</u> a great want, felt it and struggled to consummate it, come to grips with Christ as it were. But I am one of the weak. I am so weak that God has given me everything, all the tools, instructions for their use, even a good brain to use them with, a creative brain to make them immediate for others. God is feeding me and what I'm praying for is an appetite. Our Lady of Perpetual Help, pray for me.

9/25

What I am asking for is really very ridiculous. Oh Lord, I am saying, at present I am a cheese, make me a mystic, immediately. But then God can do that—make mystics out of cheeses. But why should He do it for an ingrate slothful & dirty creature like me. I can't stay in the church to say a Thanksgiving even[,] and as for preparing for Communion the night before—thoughts all elsewhere. The rosary is mere rote for me while I think of other and usually impious things. But I would like to be a mystic and immediately. But dear God please give me some place, no matter how small, but let me know it and keep it. If I am the one to wash the second step everyday, let me know it and let me wash it and let my heart overflow with love washing it. God loves us, God needs us. My soul too. So then take it dear God because it knows that You are all it should want and if it were wise You would be all it would want and the times it thinks wise, You are all it does want, and it wants more and more to want You. Its demands are absurd. It's a moth who would be king, a stupid slothful thing, a foolish thing, who wants God, who made the earth, to be its Lover. Immediately.

If I could only hold God in my mind. If I could only always just think of Him.

9/26

My thoughts are so far away from God. He might as well not have made me. And the feeling I egg up writing here lasts approximately a half hour and seems a sham. I don't want any of this artificial superficial feeling stimulated by the choir. Today I have proved myself a glutton—for Scotch oatmeal cookies and erotic thought. There is nothing left to say of me.

FACSIMILE

43

Sterling
NOTE BOOK
NO. 110

SECTION		FAMILY NAME		ROOM				GIVEN NAME		DATE	
	MON.	RM.	TUES.	RM.	WED.	RM.	THURS.	RM.	FRI.	RM.
1										
2										
3										
4										
5										
6										
7										
8										
9										
10										
11										
12										

effort at artistry in this rather than thinking of You and feeling inspired with the love I wish I had.

Dear God, I cannot love Thee the way I want to. You are the slim cresent of a moon that I see and my self is the earth's shadow that keeps me from seeing all the moon. The cresent is very beautiful and perhap that is all one like I am should or could see; but what I am afraid of, dear God, is that my self shadow will grow so large that it blocks the whole moon. and that I will judge myself by the shadow that is nothing.

I do not know You God because I am in the way. Please help me to push myself aside.

I want very much to succeed in

the world with what I want to do. I
have prayed to you about this with
my mind and my nerves on it and
strung my nerves into a tension over it
and said, "oh God please," and "I
must," and "please, please." I have
not asked you, I feel, in the right
way. Let me henceforth ask you
with resignation — that not being
or meant to be a slacking up in prayer
but a less frenzied kind — realizing
that the frenzy is caused by an
eagerness for what I want and
not a spiritual trust. I do not
wish to presume. I want to love.
Oh God please make my mind clear.
Please make it clean.
I ask you for a greater love for
my holy Mother and I ask her for

a greater love for You.

Please help me to get down under things and find where You are.

I do not mean to deny the traditional prayers I have said all my life; but I have been saying them and not feeling them. My attention is always very fugitive. This way I have it every instant. I can feel a warmth of love heating me when I think & write this to You. Please do not let the explanations of the psychologists about this make it turn suddenly cold. My intellect is so limited, Lord, that I can only trust in You to preserve me as I should be.

Please help all the ones I love to be free from their suffering. Please forgive me.

My dear God, I am impressed with how much I have to be thankful for in a material sense; and in a spiritual sense I have the opportunity of being even more fortunate. But it seems apparent to me that I am not translating this opportunity into fact. You say, dear God, to ask for grace and it will be given. I ask for it. I realize that there is more to it than that — that I have to behave like I want it. "Not those who say, Lord, Lord, but those who do the will of My Father." Please help me to know the will of my Father — not a scrupulous nervousness nor yet a lax presumption but a clear, reasonable knowlege; and after this give me a strong will to be able to ~~to~~ bend it to the Will of the Father

Please let Christian principles permeat

my writing and please let there be enough
of my writing (published) for Christian
principles to permeat. I dread, Oh Lord,
losing my faith. My mind is not strong.
It is a prey to all sorts of intellectual
quackery. I do not want it to be fear
which keeps me in the church. I don't
want to be a coward, staying with You
because I fear hell. I should reason
that if I fear hell, I can be assured of the
author of it. But learned people can
analyze for me why I fear hell and
their implication is that there is no hell.
But I believe in hell. Hell seems a
great deal more feasible to my weak
mind than heaven. No doubt because
hell is a more earthly-seeming thing. I
can fancy the tortures of the damned
but I cannot imagine the disembodied

souls hanging in a crystal for all eternity praising God. It is natural that I should not imagine this. If we could accurately map heaven some of our up-&-coming scientists would begin ~~the~~ drawing blueprints for its improvement, and the bourgeois would sell guides 10¢ the copy to all over 65. But I do not mean to be clever although I do mean to be clever on 2nd thought and like to be clever & want to be considered so. But the point more specifically here is, I don't want to fear to be out, I want to love to be in; I don't want to believe in ~~Hell~~ hell but in heaven. Stating this does me no good. It is a matter of the gift of grace. Help me to feel that I will give up every earthly thing for this. I do not mean, becoming a nun

My dear God, how stupid we people are until You give us something. Even in praying it is You who have to pray in us. I would like to write a beautiful prayer but I have nothing to do it from. There is a whole sensible world around me that I should be able to turn to Your praise; but I cannot do it. Yet at some insipid moment when I ~~might~~ may possibly be thinking of floor wax or pigeon eggs, the opening of a beautiful prayer ~~might~~ may come up from my subconscious and lead me to write something exalted. I am not a philosopher or I could understand these things.

If I knew all of myself dear God, if I could discover everything in me pedantic egocentric, in a way insincere, what would I be then? But what would I do about those feelings that are now fear,

51

now joy, that lie too deep to be touched by my understanding. I am afraid of insidious hands oh Lord which grope into the darkness of my soul. Please be my guard against them. Please be the cover at the top of the passage. Am I keeping my faith by laziness, dear God? But that is an idea that would appeal to someone who could only think.

My dear God, I do not want this to be a metaphysical exercise but something in praise of God. It is probably more liable to being therapeutic than metaphysical with the element of self underlying its thoughts. Prayers should be composed I understand of adoration, contrition, thanksgiving, and supplication and I would like to see what I can do with each without writing an exigesis. — It is the adoration of You, dear God, that most dismays me. I cannot comprehend the exaltation that must be due You. Intellectually, I assent: let us adore God. But can we do that without feeling? To feel, we must know. And for this, when it is practically impossible for us to get it ourselves, not completely, of course, but what we can, we are dependent on God. We are dependent on God ~~even for~~ our adoration of Him, adoration, that is, in the fullest sense of the term. Give me the grace, dear God, to adore You for even this I cannot do for myself. Give me the grace to adore You with the excitement of the old priests when they sacrificed a lamb to You. Give me the grace to adore

You with the awe that fills Your priests
when they sacrifice the Lamb on our
altars. Give me the grace to be impatient
for the time when I shall see You face to
face and need no stimulous than that
to adore You. Give me the grace, dear
God, to see the baseness and the misery
of the places where You are not adored
but desecrated.

Dear God, I am so discouraged about
my work. I have the feeling of discouragement that is. I realize I dont know
what I realize. Please help me dear God
to be a good writer and to get something
else accepted. That is so far from what
I deserve, of course. that I am
naturally struck with the nerve of it.

Contrition in me is largely imperfect. I don't know if I've ever been sorry for a sin because it hurt You. That kind of contrition is better than none but it is selfish. To have the other kind, it is necessary to have knowlege, faith extraordinary. All boils down to grace, I suppose. Again asking God to help us be sorry for having hurt Him. I am afraid of pain and I suppose that is what we have to have to get grace. Give me the courage to stand the pain to get the grace, Oh Lord. Help me with this life that seems so trecherous, so disappointing.

Dear God, tonight it is not disappointing because you have given me a story. Don't let me ever think, dear God, that I was

anything but the instrument for Your
story — just like the typewriter was
mine. Please let the story, dear Good,
in its revisions, be made too clear for
any false & low interpretation because
in it, I am not trying to disparage
anybodies religion although when
it was coming out, I didn't know exactly what I was trying to do or what
it was going to mean. I don't know
now if it is consistant. Please don't
let me have to scrap the story because
it turns out to mean more wrong than
right — or any wrong. I want it to
mean that the good in man is sometimes
shows through his commercialism
but that it is not the fault of the commercialism that it does.

Perhaps the idea would be that good can show through even something that is cheap. I don't know. but dear God, I wish you would take care of making it a sound story because I don't know how. just like I didn't know how to write it but it came. Anyway it all brings me to thanksgiving, the third thing to include in prayer. When I think of all I have to be thankful for I wonder that You don't just kill me now because You've done so much for me already & I haven't been particularly grateful. My thanksgiving is never in the form of self sacrifice — a few memorized prayers tattled once over lightly. All this disgusts me in myself but does not fill me with the poignant feeling I should have to adore You with, to be sorry with, or to thank You with. Perhaps the feeling I keep asking for, is something again selfish — something to help me to feel that everything with me is alright. And yet it seems only natural but maybe being thus natural is being thus selfish. My mind is a most insecure thing, not to be depended on. It gives me scruples at one minute, & leaves me lax the next. If I must know all these things thru the mind, dear Lord, please strengthen mine. Thank you, dear God, I believe & so feel thankful for all You've done for me. I want to. I do. And thank my dear Mother whom I do love, Our Lady of Perpetual Help.

My dear God, Supplication. This is the only one of the four I am competant in. It takes no supernatural grace to ask for what one wants and I have asked You bountifully, oh Lord. I believe it is right to ask You too and to ask our Mother to ak You. but I don't want to overemphasize this angle of my prayers. Help me to ask You, oh Lord, for what is good for me to have, for what I can have and do Your service by having.

I have been reading Mr. Kafka and I feel his problem of getting grace. But I see it doesn't have to be that way for the Catholic who can go to Communion everyday. The Msgr. today said it was the busi-

ness of reason, not emotion — the love
of God. The emotion would be a help.
I realized last time that it would
be a selfish one. Oh dear God, the
reason is very empty. I suppose
mine is also lazy. But I want to
get near You. Yet it seems almost
a sin to suggest such a thing even.
Perhaps ~~the~~ communion doesn't
give the nearness I mean. The
nearness I mean comes after
death perhaps. It is what we are
struggling for and if I found it
either I would be dead or I would
have seen it for a 2nd and life
would be intolerable. I don't
know about this or anything. It
sounds puerile my saying anything
so obvious.

My dear God, to keep myself on a course, I am going to consider Faith, Hope, and Charity. Now Faith. Of the three, this gives me the most mental pain. At every point in this education al process, we are told that it is ridicu- lous and their arguments sound so good it is hard not to fall into them. The arguments might not sound so good to someone with a better mind, but my mental trappings are as they are, and I am always on the brink of assenting—it is almost a subconscious assent. Now how am I to remain faithful without cowardice when these conditions influence me like they do. I can't read the particu- lar depths of myself that say something about this. There is something down there that is feeling — it is under the subconscious assent — in a certain way about this. It may be that which is holding me in. Dear God, please let it be that instead of that cowardice the psychologists would gloat so over & explain so glibly. And please don't let it be what they so jubilantly call water-tight-compartments. Dear Lord please give the people like me who don't have the brains to cope with that, please give us some kind of weapon, not to defend us from them but to defend us from ourselves after they have got through with us. Dear God, I don't want to have invented my faith to satisfy my weakness. I don't want to have

created God to my own image as they're
so fond of saying. Please give me the necessary grace, oh Lord, and please don't let
it be as hard to get as Kafka made it.

Dear God, About hope, I am somewhat at a loss. It is so easy to say
I hope to _ the tongue slides over it.
I think perhaps hope can only be
realized by contrasting it with despair.
And I am too lazy to despair. Please
don't visit me with it, dear Lord, I
would be so miserable. Hope, however, must be something distinct
from faith. I unconsciously put
it in the faith department. It must
be something positive that I have never
felt. It must be a positive force, else

why the distinction between it and faith? I would like to order things so that I can feel all of a piece spiritually. I don't suppose I order things. But all my requests seem to melt down to one for grace—that supernatural grace that does whatever it does. My mind is in a little box, dear God, down inside other boxes inside other boxes and on and on. There is very little air in my box. Dear God, please give me as much air as it is not presumptuous to ask for. Please let some light shine out of all the things around me so that I can what it amounts to I suppose is be selfish. Is there no getting around that dear God. No escape from ourselves into something bigger? Oh dear God I want to write a novel, a good novel. I want to do this for a good feeling & for a bad one. The bad one is uppermost. The psychologists say it is the natural one. Let me get away dear God from all things thus "natural." Help me to get what is more than natural into my work. Help me to love & bear with my work on that account. If I have to sweat for it, dear God, let it be as in Your service. I would like to be intelligently holy. I am a presumptuous fool, but maybe the vague thing in me that keeps me in is hope.

Dear God, in a way I got a good punishment for my lack of charity to Mr. Rothburg last year. He came back at me today like a tornado which while it didn't hurt me too much yet ruined my show. All this is about charity. Dear Lord please make my mind vigilant about that. I say many many too many uncharitable things about people everyday, I say them because they make me look clever. Please help me to realize practically how cheap this is. I have nothing to be proud of yet myself. I am stupid, quite as stupid as the people I ridicule. Please help me to stop this selfishness because I love you, dear God.

I don't want to be all excuses though
I am not much. Please help me to
do Your Word oh Lord.

11/4

I have decided this is not much as a
direct medium of prayer. Prayer is not
even as premeditated as this — it is of the
moment & this is too slow for the moment.
I have started on a new phase of my
spiritual life — I trust. Tied up with
it, is the throwing off of certain adolescent habits & habits of mind. It
does not take much to make us realize
what fools we are, but the little it
takes is long in coming. I see my
ridiculous self by degrees. One thing
I have seen this week — it has been
a peculiar week — is my constant
seeing of myself as what I want to be

not the fulfillment of what I want
to be, but the right genre, the correct
embryo in the correct beast. The consequence ~~s~~ of such a delightful state
of coma ~~~~ will naturally be the ~~fetus~~
~~fetual~~ eternal embryo — and eternal
in no false sense. I must grow.
I have a right I believe to show
such interest in myself as long as
my interest is in my immortal soul
and what keeps it pure. "Save to
the pure & in their purest hour,"
Coleridge wrote — the gift of imagination functioned only then,
only for those. Start with the soul
and perhaps the temporal gifts
I want to exercise will have their
chance; and if they do not, I
have the best in my hands already,

the only thing really needed. God
must be in all my work. I have
been reading Bernanos. It is so
very wonderful. Will I ever know
anything?

11/61

Mediocrity is a hard word to apply to
oneself; yet I see myself so equal with
it that it is impossible not to throw it
at myself — realizing even as I do that
I will be old & beaten before I accept it.
I think to accept it would be to accept
Despair. There must be some way for
the naturally mediocre to escape it.
The way must be Grace. There must be
a way to escape it even when you know
you are even below it. Perhaps knowing
you are below it is a way to begin. I
say I am equal with it; but I am

below it. I will always be staggering between Despair & Presumption, facing first one & then the other, deciding which makes me look the best, which fits most comfortably, most conveniently. I'll never take a large chunk of anything. I'll nibble nervously here & there. ~~Fear of God~~ is right; but, God, it is not this nervousness. It is something huge, great, magnanimous. It must be a joy. Every virtue must be vigorous. Virtue must be the only vigorous thing in our lives. Sin is large & stale. You can never finish eating it nor ever digest it. It has to be vomited. But perhaps that is too literary a ~~dramatic~~ statement — this musn't get insincere.

How can I live — how shall I live. Obviously the only way to live right is to give up everything. But I have no vocation + maybe that is wrong anyway. But how eliminate this picky fish bone kind of way I do things. I want so to love God all the way. At the same time I want all the things that seem opposed to it — I want to be a _fine_ writer. Any success will tend to swell my head — unconsciously even. If I ever do get to be a fine writer, it will not be because I am a fine writer but because God has ~~used be~~ given me credit for a few of the things He kindly wrote for me. Right at present this does not seem to be His policy. I can't write a thing. But I'll continue to try —

that is the point. And at every dry point, I will be reminded Who is doing the work when it is done & Who is not doing it at that moment. Right now I wonder if God will ever do any more writing for me. He has promised His grace; I am not so sure about the other. Perhaps I have not been thankful enough for what has gone before.

The desires of the flesh — excluding the stomach — have been taken away from me. For how long I don't know but I hope forever! It is a great peace to be rid of them.

Can't anyone teach me how to pray?

11/11

How hard it is to keep any one intention
any one attitude toward a piece of work
any one tone any one anything. I
find a certain peace in my soul these
days that is very fine - lead us not into
temptation. The story level, bah.
Work, work, work. Dear God, let
me work, keep me working, I want
so to be able to work. If my sin is
laziness I want to be able to conquer
it & I looked back over some of these
entries.

1/2/47

No one can be an atheist who does not know all things. Only God is an atheist. The devil is the greatest believer & he has his reasons.

1/11/47

Can we ever settle on calling ourselves mediocre— me on myself? If I am not this or that that someone else is, may I not be something else that I am that I cannot yet see fully or describe? I go back, and

7 St. Thomas

74

Rousseau has it that the Protestant has to think; the Catholic to submit. It is presumed I suppose that ultimately the Protestant ~~too~~ has to submit; but the Catholic never to think, i.e., about ~~his~~ the nature of man's relation to God. This is interesting. Catholicism being a guide book to the only means of communication is worth submitting ~~to~~ ~~for~~ in the Catholic's view. And all these doctrines which deny submission deny God. Hell, a literal hell, is our only hope. Take it away & we will become ~~what we~~ wholly a wasteland not a half a one. Sin is a great thing as long as its recognized. It leads a good many people to God who wouldn't get there otherwise. But cease to recognize it, or take it away from devil as devil & give it to devil as psychologist, and you also take away God. If there is no sin ~~in this world~~ there is no God in heaven. no heaven.

There are those who would have it that way.
But even among the literary now it is
becoming popular to believe in ~~a~~ God.
There is a certain shocking something
about it. But Catholics have to think
certainly - as far as they are able - or as far
maybe as they want to only. Me. I have
to in an attempt to do this and trying to
shock with God? Am I trying to push
Him in there violently, feet foremost? Maybe
that's alright. Maybe if I'm doing it
its allright? Maybe I'm mediocre. I'd
rather be less. I'd rather be nothing. An
imbecile. Yet this is wrong. Mediocrity,
if that is my scourge, is something I'll
have to submit to. If that is my
scourge. If I ever find out will be
time to submit. I will have to have a
good many opinions.

1/25/47

The majesty of my thoughts this evening! Do
all these things read alike as they seem to? They
all send a faint nausea thru me – albeit they
were sincere at the time & I recant none of my
articles of faith. This evening I picture theoretically myself at 70 saying it's done, it's finished, it's
what it is, & being no nearer than I am. This
moral turpitude at 70 won't be tolerable. I want
a revolution now, a mild revolution, something
that will put a now 20th cen. acesticism into me at
least when I pass the grocery.

The intellectual & artistic delights God gives
us are visions – like visions we pay for them, &
The thirst for the vision doesn't necessarily
carry with it a thirst for the attendent suffering.
Looking back I have suffered, not my share, but
enough to call it that but there's a terrific balance
due. Dear God please send me Your Grace.

4/14/47

I must write down that I am to be an artist. Not in the sense of aesthetic frippery but in the sense of aesthetic craftsmanship; otherwise I will feel my lonliness continually like this today. The word craftsmanship takes care of the work angle & the word aesthetic the truth angle. Angle. It will be a ~~continual~~ life struggle with no consumation. When something is finished, it cannot be possessed. Nothing can be possessed but the struggle. All our lives are consumed in possessing struggle but only when the struggle is cherished & directed to a final consumation outside of this life is it of any value. I want to be the best artist it is possible for me to be, under God.

I do not want to be lonely all my life
but people only make us lonlier by
reminding us of God. Dear God please
help me to be an artist, please let it
lead to You.

5/4

To maintain any thread in the novel there must
be a view of the world behind it & the most important single item under this view of world is
conception of love — divine, natural, & perverted
It is probably possible to say that when a
view of love is present — a broad enough view —
no more need be added to make the world view.
Freud, Proust, Lawrence have located love
inside the human & there is no need to
question their location; however, there is
no need either to define love as they do —
only as desire; since this precludes

79

Divine Love, which, while it too may be desire, is a different kind of desire — Divine desire — and is outside of men and capable of lifting him up to itself. Man's desire for God is bedded in his unconscious & seeks to satisfy itself in physical possession of another human. This necessarily is a passing, fading attatchment in its sensuous aspects since it's a poor substitute for what the unconscious is after. The more conscious the desire for God becomes the more successful union with another becomes because the intelligence realizes the relation in its relation to a greater desire & if this intelligence is ~~not~~ ~~doubles greatis~~ the motive power in the desire for God becomes double & gains in becoming God-like. The modern man isolated from faith, from raising his desire for God into a conscious desire, is sunk into the position of seeing physical love as an end in itself. Thus his romanti-cizing it, wallowing in it, & then cynicizing it. Or in the case of the artist like Proust of his realizing that it is the only thing worth life but seeing it without purpose, accidental, and unsatisfying after desire has been fulfiled. Proust's conception of ~~desire~~ could only be that way since he makes it the highest point of existence — which it is — but with nothing supernatural to end in. It sinks lower & lower in the unconscious, to the very pit of it, which is Hell. Certainly hell is located in the unconscious even as the desire for God is. The desire for God may be in a super-consciousness which is unconscious. Satan fell into his libido or his id whichever is the more complete Freudian term

Perversion is the end result of denying
or revolting against supernatural love,
descending from the unconscious super-
consciousness to the id. Where perversion is disease or result of disease, this
does not apply since no free will operates. The
Sex act is a religious act & when it occurs
without God it is a mock act or at best an
empty act. Proust is right that only a
love which does not satisfy can continue.
Two people can remain "in love" — a
phrase made practically useless by
stinking romanticism — only if their
common desire for each other unites in
a greater desire for God — i.e., they do
not become satisfied but more desirous
together of the supernatural love in union
with God — My God, take these boils &
blisters & warts of sick romanticism

5/30

Wore the last thing out. It was worthy
of me all right; but not worthy of what
I ought to be. Bloy has come my way.
The awful thing is that we can go back
to ourselves being ourselves after reading
him. He is an iceburg hurled at me
to break up my Titanic and I hope my
Titanic will be smashed, but I am
afraid it takes more than Bloy to destroy
the age in us — the age is The Fall still
I suppose and certainly Original Sin
in us. Conquer it but can't throw
it off; fight it and maim it but never
kill it. It is hard to want to suffer; I
presume Grace is necessary for the want.
I am a mediocre of the spirit but there
is hope. I am at least of the spirit and
that means alive. What about these

dead people I am living with, what about them? We who live will have to pay for their deaths. Being dead what can they do. It is for them, I presume, that the saints died. No, the saints died for God and God died for the dead. They didn't have to submit to God's indignity. No one can do again what Christ did. These modern "Christs" pictured on war posters & in poems — "every man is Jesus; every woman Mary" would have made Bloy retch. The rest of us have lost our power to vomit.

9/22 and Bloy again. It should be a great instigator of humility in me that I am so lukewarm as to need Bloy always & send me into serious thought — and even then it is not sustained very long. The summer was very arid spiritually & up here getting & go to Mass again everyday has left me unmoved — thoughts awful in their pettyness & selfishness come into my mind even with the Host on my tongue. Maybe the Lord had pity on me and sent me wandering down the stacks to pick up Pfleger on Bloy & Péguy and some others. It is terrible to think of my unconsciousness when I really know. Too weak to pray for suffering too weak even to get out a prayer for anything much except trifles. I don't want to be doomed to mediocrity in my feeling for Christ. I want to feel. I want to love. Take me, dear Lord, and set me in the direction I am to go. My Lady of Perpetual Help, pray for me.

Dear Lord please make me want
You. It would be the greatest
bliss. Not just to want You
when I think about You but
to want You all the time, to think
about You all the time, to have
the want driving in me, to have it
like a cancer in me. It would
kill me like a cancer and that
would be the Fullfillment. It is
easy for this writing to show a
want. There is a want but it is
abstract and cold, a dead want
that goes well into writing because
writing is dead. Writing is dead.
Art is dead, dead by nature, not
killed by unkindness. I bring
my dead want into the place

the dead place it shows up most
easily, into writing. This has its
purpose if by God's grace it will
wake another soul, but it does
me no good. The life it receives
in writing is dead to me, the more
so in that it looks alive — a horrible
deception. But not to me who
knows this. Oh Lord please make
this dead desire living, living
in life, living as it will probably
have to live in suffering. I feel
too mediocre now to suffer. If
suffering came to me I would
not even recognize this it. Lord
keep me. Mother help me.

Giving one Catholicity, God deprives
one of the pleasure of looking for it
but here again He has shown His
mercy for such a one as myself and
for that matter for all contemporary
Catholics who, if it had not been
given, would not have looked forth
It is certainly His provision for
all mediocre souls — a tool for us.
For Bloy's statue it is — how to call
it? God on earth? God as nearly as we
can get to Him on earth. I wish only
that I were one of the strong. If I
were that less would have been given
me and I would have felt a great
want, felt it and struggled to
consummate it, come to grips with
Christ as it were. But I am one

of the weak. I am so weak that God has given me everything, all the tools, instructions for their use, even a good brain to use them with, a creative brain to make them immediate for others. God is feeding me and what I'm praying for is an appitite. Our Lady of Perpetual Help, pray for me.

9/25

What I am asking for is really very ridiculous. Oh Lord, I am saying, at present I am a cheeze, make me a mystic, immediately. But then God can do that — make mystics out of cheezes. But why should He do it for an ingrate slothful + dirty creature like me. I can't stay in the church

to say a Thanksgiving even and
as for preparing for Communion
the night before — thoughts all
elsewhere. The rosary is mere rote
for me while I think of other and
usually impious things. But
I would like to be a mystic and
immediately. But dear God
please give me some place, no
matter how small, but let me
know it and keep it. If I am
the one to wash the second step
everyday, let me know it and
let me wash it and let my heart
overflow with love washing it. God
loves us, God needs us. My soul too.
So then take it dear God because
it knows that You are all it
should want and if it were

wise You would be all it would want
and the times it thinks wise, You
are all it does want, and it wants
more and more to want You. Its
demands are absurd It's a
moth who would be king, a stupid
slothful thing, a foolish thing,
who wants ~~the~~ God who made the
earth, to be its Lover. Immediately.
If I could only hold God in my
mind. If I could only always
just think of Him.

9/26

My thoughts are so far away from
God ~~He~~ might as well not have made
me. ~~And~~ This feeling I egg up
writing here lasts approximately
a half hour and seems a sham.
I don't want any of this artificial

superficial feeling stimulated
by the choir.   Today I have
proved myself a glutton—for
both oat meal cookies and erotic
thought. There is nothing left to
say of me.

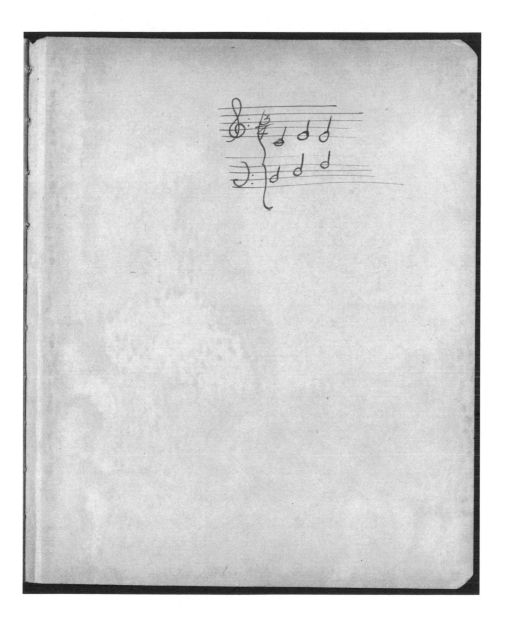

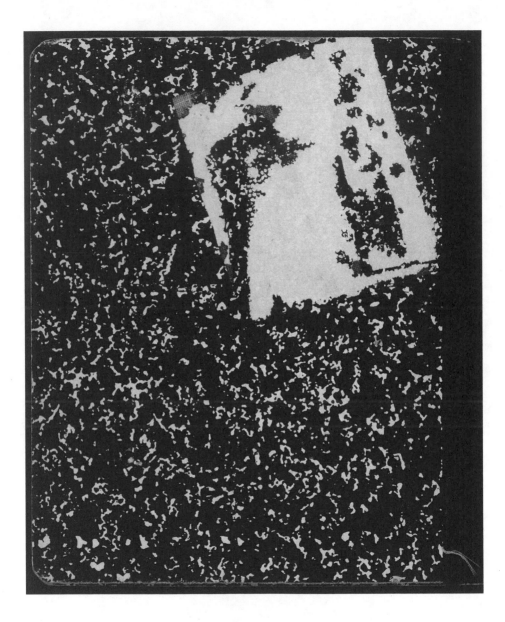